The Death Of Money

The Prepper's Survival Guide To The Loss Of Paper Wealth And How To Survive An Economic Collapse

By Ron Johnson

Copyright©2014 Ron Johnson
This book or any portion thereof may not be reproduced or used in any way whatsoever without the written consent of the Author except for the purpose of brief quotations for book reviews.

Disclaimer

This book is intended to be a general guide, to raise awareness, and to help people make informed decisions in the context of their own personal circumstance.

The author accepts no responsibility for any loss or injury be it personal or financial, as a result for the use or misuse of the information in this book. If you have any doubts or concerns after reading this book, please speak to a qualified person before taking any actions.

Contents

Introduction

Chapter 1

What Could Possibly Cause Of An Economic Collapse?

Chapter 2

What Usually Happens When Money Becomes Worthless

Chapter 3

How To Survive If Your Money Or Paper Assets Become Worthless

Chapter 4

How To Survive Without Money

Conclusion

Introduction

Have you ever thought about what you would do when the money in your pocket becomes worthless? You scoff at the idea, but it is a very real possibility. The dollar, the yen, the euro and every other currency are all on shaky ground. The world as we know it is built upon empty promises and pipe dreams. You could say we have grown too big for our britches. In an attempt to stimulate a fledgling economy, countries have printed more money hoping it will make consumers spend more. The money is paper and about as valuable as paper. There is no gold reserves to back it up.

We keep writing checks with the hope we can borrow money from somebody else before the check clears. The loan comes in and we don't have enough so we take another loan and then another loan and there is still no revenue coming in to cover the repayment of the multiple loans. This is the situation that is happening in various governments around the world. Banks are loaning money they don't have and borrowing from lenders to cover the loans. Imagine if every person went to the bank to withdraw their savings. It wouldn't be there!

The powers that be refuse to believe the economy is in the toilet. If they admit the problem, there will be political backlash as citizens rebel and demand the governments tighten up the purse strings and stop the bleeding. Unfortunately, it will never happen. We have seen that time and again. The only way our governments will admit the problem is when they hit rock bottom. It isn't just a possibility. It is a probability based on history, which we will discuss in the next chapter.

Rock bottom will mean the death of paper money. Are you prepared to live in a world where the money in the bank is worthless? A world where you cannot buy the things you want and need because paper money is no more valuable than the paper in a notebook. What about a job? You won't have a job because money is worthless! It is nearly inconceivable to truly imagine a world without paper money, but it is something every citizen in every country should think about.

Can you get by? Don't be embarrassed if you answer no. Most people would be lost. That is why you need this book. You need this book to plan for a future without money. You can still thrive and the world will rebuild, but in the meantime, you need to know how to survive.

Chapter 1

What Could Possibly Cause an Economic Collapse?

What could happen that would result in such devastation? You may be surprised to know there are numerous scenarios that could cause paper money to become worthless. It isn't just a single situation. With so many different reasons, it confirms the need to be prepared for the end of cash. The risks are intensified. It just makes sense you would prepare to do without money and to survive on your own wits. Any single event would cause people to lose jobs. Most people are only two pay checks away from financial ruin. Within a month of businesses going under, the economy would start to crumble with mortgages, credit cards and loans defaulting.

Major Market Crash

A major collapse of the markets around the world can happen and has happened in the past. Sure, we managed to pull out of the slump, but the economy has never fully recovered. We are hanging on by our fingertips. All it takes is a single disaster, act of war or a major business going under to send the market into turmoil. A major crash would devastate the economy.

A typical bank run which as a result of the Wall St crash of 1929 ruined and displaced millions of people around the world

Businesses would be forced to close, people would lose their jobs and we would see something akin to The Great Depression.

Anybody who has invested in stocks would lose money. People who have retired and put their retirement funds in stocks would be broke and unable to survive. A major crash would have a ripple effect that would eventually turn the entire world upside down.

Hyperinflation

Hyperinflation is something we have seen before. When regulatory agencies recognize the signs of an economic collapse, they do what they can to stop it. They print more money with the idea that more money will help stimulate the economy and set things back to rights. Nope. That doesn't work. It creates hyperinflation. More money is truly more problems. More money printed means the money that is in your pocket is pretty much worthless.

A 500 billion Yugoslav dinar note from the Former Yugoslavia's period of hyperinflation between 1989 and 1994

That loaf of bread you normally pay a dollar for is now going to cost you fifty dollars, but you still only have a dollar. Hyperinflation is when goods and services increase in price at a staggering rate. Hyperinflation is common in the aftermath of a war. Citizens have lost all faith in their government and don't want to feed it by spending money. Citizens and business owners don't trust the money and want a whole lot of it just to make sure they are making a profit from whatever goods or services they are selling.

Deflation

Deflation is essentially the opposite of hyperinflation. On the surface, deflation looks great for consumer. That same loaf of bread we talked about in the hyperinflation drops in price to let's say .50 cents a loaf. Now you can two loaves for the price of one. That sounds like an excellent deal. Unfortunately, when deflation sticks around for too long, businesses start to lose money. Their profits drop, which means there are going to be doors closed and jobs lost. It doesn't matter how much the bread is if you don't have a job to earn income to buy the bread.

Deflation is one thing government can't control no matter how much money they throw at it. It is thought to be one of the worst possible scenarios to happen to the economy. Short-term deflation is not too bad and businesses can recover. It is the long-term deflation situations that leave companies in the red.

Natural Disaster

A natural disaster that devastates a large area of the country could have long lasting negative impacts on the economy. It isn't unheard of for a strong tornado, hurricane or earthquake to cause billions of dollars of damage. If there were more than a single massive storm in a short period of time, it could disrupt the entire economy. A hurricane in Florida and an earthquake in California would send America into a tailspin. Government aid would be depleted and insurance companies would not have the available funds to pay out. People in the hardest hit areas would not have jobs to go to. They would default on their loans, which would have a major impact on the banks. The ripple effect would be extensive and a major economic collapse would ensue.

Historical Examples

The following are just two historical examples of a time when a government's paper money became absolutely worthless. These examples are why it is important for you to pay attention and realize that another collapse is inevitable.

Zimbabwe

Zimbabwe has been in so decline since the early 2000s. Recently, the economy has taken a severe downturn that has had a ripple effect. As the economy started to tank, citizens were losing their jobs at an alarming rate. In 2014, the unemployment rate was around 90 percent. Imagine, 9 out of every 10 people jobless. Jobless and unable to pay their bills, buy things and do what is necessary to stimulate an economy. The economic circle was broken and repair of the economy looks impossible. The Zimbabwe economy was sent into a tailspin following the involvement in the war involving the

Plies of worthless Zimbabwean dollars

Republic of the Congo back in 1998 until 2002. War is expensive and it will always strain a country's finances. Hyperinflation slammed Zimbabwe's economy in 2003 and held on until 2009 when the country finally suspended their money in an effort to stop the bleeding. The Zimbabwe currency was absolutely worthless and it was taken off the market in favour of the American dollar. This is a situation that started out slow and quickly spiralled out of control, which is the point of this book.

Germany

After World War I Germany was left in serious financial trouble. Germany's collapse in the 1920s was the precursor the The Great Depression. Germany was ordered to make reparation payments to Great Britain and France, which they couldn't afford. The economy struggled for over 10 years before it finally crumbled under the strain. Germany tried to combat the steady decline and began printing money to stimulate the economy. This sent them into hyperinflation. It wasn't long before the United States tumbled into financial distress as well. They tried to demand repayment of the loans to try and fix their own failed economy, which only depressed the German economy further. It was a recipe for financial disaster.

German banknotes were worth so little during German's period of hyperinflation in the 1920's that people were using it as wall paper

Chapter 2

What Usually Happens When Money Becomes Worthless

Scenes such as witnessed during the Greek protests over austerity would be more widespread in a global economic collapse

When a country's currency finally fails, there is a fallout like none other. The ripple effects are widespread and it will affect currencies in other countries. Imagine the world climbing a mountain together on the same length of rope. When one of the countries near the top of the rope starts to slip, it will take down the entire length. This is what has happened in the past and experts are convinced it will happen again.

Money devalues for various reasons. A lot of the responsibility of the value of a particular currency is based on what investors deem valuable. Investors who start to get cold feet will abruptly pull their money from a particular sector and demand loans be repaid. The panic spreads and other investors assume something is wrong and demand the same repayment. To repay the loans, the countries must try to make money by increasing their exports. But, people are not going to buy what they are selling if they don't lower their prices to make the goods more desirable. They lower prices and cut profits with the hopes of making more money. They have to cut labour costs to try and keep the balance and begin laying off workers and do some cost cutting to get the most out of the exports. This results in lower productivity, a decrease in exports and a major financial crisis.

When currency loses its value, it sets off a string of events that will leave the country crippled and the citizens fighting for survival.

- Gold and silver will be the truest forms of money
- Bartering will become the new currency
- Jobs will be lost and people will have to be self-sufficient
- Commodities like food, water and ammunition will be the new cash
- Unemployment will skyrocket
- Civil unrest will ensue

The devaluation of paper money will have a domino effect. It isn't likely everything would happen in a matter of days. You will have some warning it is happening and will be able to move out of the city to a more secure, rural location and prepare for the worst.

- People will start losing jobs in large numbers as major companies close their doors
- Unemployment will hit some of the highest numbers ever seen
- Government aid will be taxed as the unemployed try to get assistance—it will be cut back and ultimately dry up
- Government services will be dramatically cut
- Healthcare will be limited as hospitals lose funding and clinics don't get paid
- Transportation will grind to a halt, city buses will lose

funding, airlines will go broke
- Gas will be limited as deliveries stop
- Supply chains will be interrupted and eventually cease, store shelves will be empty of food and other necessities
- Necessities will increase in price by huge jumps, making them unaffordable for most of the unemployed
- Electricity will eventually be shut off—nobody can pay their bills and the companies will be unable to pay their employees
- Schools will shutter their doors with no funding to pay teachers or bills
- Civil unrest, looting and violence will plague cities as people struggle to survive.

Life as we know it would cease to exist within a year. These things won't happen overnight, but they will happen. If you are not prepared to live without electricity or to survive with the food you have in your pantry, your life is going to be extremely difficult.

The Historical Precedents

We know paper money is going to fail. A look back at history reveals that nearly every form of paper currency becomes worthless at some point. Typically, a new currency is put into place, but it can take months or years for that to happen. Research shows 599 paper currencies have come and gone throughout the history of money. That is a staggering amount and cements the idea that paper money in today's world will follow suit. Of that number, 156 were destroyed by hyperinflation. Hyperinflation is the death knell of any currency. This should be taken as a warning sign. The moment hyperinflation begins; it is time to start preparing for the end of paper money.

Another startling statistic is 165 of those now defunct currencies were destroyed by war. Wars that conquer a nation or deplete a nation's funds are going to kill paper currency. The nation will either be absorbed by another country and assume that currency or come up with a new form.

History also reveals that most currency only manages to stay in circulation about 39 years. The American dollar has surpassed that age by a few years, but it is safe to say it is on shaky ground. Is the end of the dollar just around the corner?

If the American dollar fails, the nation will be unable to pay back the trillions of dollars of debt to other countries. Those countries will topple as they struggle to cope with one of the economic leaders of the world bottoming out. Poverty will be the new norm. People will be forced to beg, borrow and steal what they need to survive. It will truly be an end to life as we know it.

We won't be able to run to the store to buy a gallon of milk and a loaf of bread. Instead, we will have to either have our own dairy cow or be able to trade with a person who does. Bread will have to be baked, but you probably wouldn't have electricity to do so. America and the rest of the developed world will be tossed back into third-world status. Very few people will know how to cope or how to survive.

Life will be difficult and those who have not prepared to survive such a calamity are going to either die or resort to violent means to get what they do need.

Chapter 3

How to Survive If Your Money or Paper Assets Become Worthless

You don't want to be one of those people who gets caught off guard when money becomes worthless. Those folks are destined to a short life full of strife. You want to be prepared. To survive, you have to spend some time learning new skills and stocking up on things that will aid in survival, like food. You can't survive without spending some time preparing.

Preppers who are doing what they can today, when money can buy them food, ammunition and other necessities are going to be the wealthy ones when the economy collapses. They will have what they need to maintain a fairly normal existence without being forced to hurt others to get what they need.

The Skills You Should Learn

Because you are going to be surviving on your own wits, you need to learn some skills that will aid in your survival. Keep in mind, there won't be any stores for you to buy things you need. You have to figure out a way to make it yourself. You won't be able to pick up the phone and call for a pizza delivery or even an ambulance should you find yourself in a medical emergency. You are on your own. You have to be a jack of all trades.

The following are some skills you should learn and practice today to prepare for a future that most definitely does not look bright.

- First aid training will be crucial for you to know. You will need to know what to do to stop heavy bleeding, stitch up minor wounds and how to perform CPR. It would be a good idea for you to take a first aid class through your local Red Cross or college. The knowledge you learn in these classes could very well save the life of a loved one. Being able to perform first aid will be invaluable and in world where money has no value, a skill such as this would be extremely valuable.
- Gardening and farming are going to be your grocery store. You need to learn how to grow bountiful crops. Learning how to grow food through the winter months will also be crucial. There is some skill involved to growing your own food. You cannot expect to throw some seeds in the ground and hope for the best. You have to learn how to combat disease and pests as well as how to properly fertilize and water your crops.
- Preserving food will also be extremely important. Your summer and fall harvests will have to carry you throughout the year until the next harvest. You must learn how to dry food, store root crops in a root cellar and even learn to can food to make it last.
- Chopping wood is going to be necessary to heat your home, clean your water and cook your meals. You need to know how to find good firewood and chop it safely. Hauling the wood back to your home is going to be a real chore. Buying a cart that will help you with the task can make your life much easier.
- Raising livestock will also be an important skill to know. You will need food other than what comes

from your garden. Chickens, pigs and even goats are small enough they won't require a lot of room and are fairly easy to raise. Learning the ins and outs of raising livestock will ensure you have food on the table when times are tough.
- Hunting will be necessary if you are not raising livestock or your livestock has died from disease or been stolen. Learning how to hunt with a gun is great, but ammunition may be in short supply. It is a good idea to learn how to set traps and snares as well as how to hunt with a bow and arrow.
- Sewing by hand will also prove to be invaluable when the mall is shut down and you can't buy new clothes. You will have to know how to take what you have and turn it into what you need. Mending socks and repairing torn in-seams will become the norm instead of buying new socks or pants.
- Knitting will be an extremely valuable skill. Knitting your own clothing as well as items to barter with is going to be very useful. Stock up on yarn and stash it away.
- Self-defence skills will be a priority. You are going to have to protect what you have. Shooting interlopers is not always going to be your best option. You will need to learn some basic defence skills that will help you fight off anybody who tries to take what you have.

How to Strengthen Your Position

When the economy collapses and paper money is worthless, you are probably going to have to hole up somewhere, preferably out of town and on a nice piece of land. Once you get where you are going, it is time to hunker down and strengthen your position. You need to prepare for the onslaught of those who didn't prepare and want what you have. You have to be ready to defend what is yours.

To strengthen your position, you need to do several things. The following list includes some suggestions for you to use to make your dwelling a little safer and less appealing to looters and various ragamuffins.

- Do your best to make your dwelling look ransacked, dishevelled and abandoned. You don't want to have a neatly tended lawn with flowers growing in pots on the front stoop. That shows somebody is living there and somebody is clearly thriving. Sorry about the neighbourhood, but it is important you "trash up" your front yard. Throw some garbage around the yard and add in some old clothing as well. Burn some spots in the grass and under the windows to give the appearance the home has been burned out and not worth stopping by to look for anything good.
- Board up the windows and the front door. You want to do your best to stop people from coming in. Make it difficult and some of the lazy looters will walk on by.
- Set up early warning signals to alert you to potential intruders. It is best to head them off before they can get into your home. Wires run along the ground and attached to tin cans or bells are one way to give you a heads up somebody is coming. If you know somebody is coming, you can stop them before they get through the front door.
- Put up signs letting intruders know you are armed and will do what is necessary to protect you and yours. If you have one of these signs, be prepared to

back it up.
- If you are feeling really macabre, you could spill animal blood, ketchup or tomato sauce in the driveway, fence post or front porch to make your house super scary looking.

What You Should Stockpile

You need to start stockpiling some goods today to prepare for that dreadful day when money becomes worthless. You have your work cut out for you here. It takes months; possibly years to build up a stockpile of food and other supplies that will carry you for at least a year following the day money dies. This is a list of things you need to start stockpiling today. It is going to take some time so there is no time like the present to get started.

Water
- Store as much drinking water as possible, gallon jugs, bottled water
- Store water in large rain barrels
- Store water in cisterns or dig an area for a pond if possible
- Water purification tablets
- Water filtration systems
- Bleach to purify water
- Portable water containers

Food
- Canned soup
- Canned chilli, spaghetti, ravioli and etc...
- Ramen noodles

- Dried beans
- Grains i.e. oats, rice, flour, cornmeal
- Freeze-dried foods, meals are a good option
- Canned meats
- Coffee
- Tea
- Sugar
- Spices; salt, pepper and herbs
- Cereals
- Cooking oil
- Freeze-dried dairy cheese, milk, butter
- Crackers
- Pastas
- Tomato sauce, pasta sauce
- Peanut butter
- Jams, jellies
- Protein bars
- Dried fruits, fruit leathers
- Granola
- Baking ingredients, baking soda, baking powder, yeast
- Honey
- Chocolate, bars and powder
- Heirloom seeds—to grow your own garden

Personal Hygiene Items
- Soap
- Toothpaste, toothbrushes, floss
- Feminine hygiene items
- Hand sanitizer
- Toilet paper
- Shampoo

- Baby diapers—if needed
- Wet wipes
- Bug spray
- Sunscreen
- Chapstick
- Razors

Gear and Tools
- Hammer and nails
- Basic tool kit, screwdrivers, wrenches and etc...
- Duct tape
- Sharp knives
- Gardening tools i.e. shovel, hoe, rake
- Rope, paracord
- Axe
- Handsaw
- Lantern—solar is best
- Flash light—solar powered is best, if not extra batteries
- Fishing pole and tackle
- Compass
- 5-gallon buckets
- Emergency candles
- Tarps or heavy plastic sheeting

Kitchen Items
- Cast iron cookware
- Manual tools i.e. can opener, blender, mixer
- Solar oven
- Percolated coffee maker
- Disposable utensils (for times when water is in short supply)

- Garbage bags—lots of garbage bags!
- Aluminium foil
- Ziploc bags
- Teapot with handle to hang over open fire

Medical Supplies
- Rolls of gauze
- Band-aids in varying sizes
- Triple antibiotic ointment
- Pain relievers
- Ace bandages
- Gauze pads
- Raw Honey—an excellent antibiotic and healing agent
- Antihistamine
- Gloves—neoprene are best in case of an allergy to latex
- Fish antibiotics—when antibiotics are not available
- A book about homoeopathic and natural medicine
- Basic suture kits
- Antacids

Miscellaneous
- Entertainment—you will get mighty bored without electricity or a job to go to. Having plenty of books, puzzles, board games and other hobby ideas will keep you and the family entertained.
- Pet food is important if you plan on keeping your family dog or cat with you.
- Self-defence items, knives, guns and ammo, pepper spray or a taser will help you fight off people intent on taking your supplies.
- Plenty of warm clothing and blankets—you can never

have too many blankets. Buy them now while they are on sale and inexpensive.
- Fire extinguishers—without a fire department you need to be able to put out any fires before they destroy your home.
- Gold and silver coins will likely be useful. Avoid buying bars of gold or silver. It isn't like a person can make change. If you are using a silver coin to purchase a few rolls of toilet paper, you want to make sure you are getting a good deal.

Don't wait to start buying things when you see the signs of an economic collapse. It will be too late. You need to buy items when they are plentiful and more affordable. Buying a single flash light and an extra pack of batteries isn't going to help you if the situation lasts for more than a week. You need to stock up on everything on the above lists. Once you have one of everything, it is time to start bulking up. Food and the tools necessary for survival should be your priority. If you can't store water, you absolutely must store a way to make water you do find safe to drink.

Chapter 4

How to Survive Without Money

Without money, life is going to be very strange for us. We have become so used to buying what we want and need with paper money. We go to work to pay our bills and buy food for the family. When all of that is gone, you are going to be left feeling a little adrift. What do you do with your days? How do you keep a roof over your family's head? How do you feed them?

It is a bit overwhelming when think of a life without money, but it can be done. You will have to get used to a new normal and a new way of living. When you are prepared, the transition will be much easier. You and your family will thrive in a post-economic collapse world. Life will be a little harder, but in many ways, you may actually enjoy it more. When you are unplugged from the world and are forced to use your hands and spend time with your family, you are actually gaining something a little more important. You are passing down valuable skills to your children. You are learning more about your family members than you ever would have if you continued to communicate via text messages and those few precious moments in the morning before everybody set off for work and school.

Our ancestors managed to survive with very little money. They used a different system to get what they needed. Think back to the days when folks lived out on prairies or far out in the country. They didn't run to the store every week. They couldn't because they didn't have "real" jobs, which meant they didn't have any cash flow. But they still managed to get the necessities. How? Bartering.

Bartering will be the new tender. Bartering for goods and services is one of the oldest forms of currency and it is always going to be around. It is our fail safe in an uncertain world. You can call it trading, but it is basically the same concept. You have a skill or a bag of potatoes that your neighbour needs and he has toilet paper that you need. You trade straight across. Everybody is happy and no money was exchanged.

How to Barter

If you are unfamiliar with bartering, and most of us are, you need to know the ins and outs of bartering. One of the most important issues is determining how much something is worth. It isn't like there is going to be a tag on a particular item indicating it costs 3 tomatoes or 2 rolls of toilet paper. Bartering is something that is going to depend on what it is, the availability of the item and how bad you want it.

Bartering is all about negotiation. Ideally, you would only want to barter with a person who is relatively honest and trustworthy. You don't want to end up with a pot of bad beans that you paid for with your last pack of bandages.

Bartering has its risks, but it is the only way to get what you want and need when money isn't an option.

The key to getting a good deal is to practice your poker face. If somebody knows you really want or need something, they will charge you more because they can, not because the item is actually worth anything more. Bartering "prices" are based on need and demand. For example, the flat screen television you have isn't going to be worth as much as a case of canned chilli simply because there is no need for a television when there is no electricity.
If you have an obvious injury and you need bandages and the person you are bartering with sees your need, they are going to demand more for the bandages than if you were hale and hearty. The key is to feign disinterest. If it doesn't appear you have to have a specific item, the person you are trading with knows you are not going to barter something of relative value, like a bottle of vodka.

In a post-economic collapse, it is up to you and the folks you are trading with to determine the value of a particular item. Food, water, flash lights and other survival gear is going to be worth a lot. How much depends on whether there is more food around the corner or if you are holding the very last can of food in a 10-mile radius.
Luxury items are going to be of supreme value. Luxuries are just that. If they are not necessary for survival and are simply a way to be a little more comfortable, they are going to be very valuable. Think of the luxury cars today compared to a basic car. The luxury cars are more expensive simply because they are a little more posh. The cars both do the same thing and get a person from point A to point B, but it is the little extras that make it desirable. A Snickers bar is going to more desirable than a can of green beans, which will make it more valuable. Both are food, but

a Snickers bar would certainly taste a lot better than green beans.

Never reveal how much of a particular item you have—that will devalue it. If you have stumbled across a truck load of canned beans, you don't want to advertise it for two reasons. For one, if people know beans are in great supply, they are not worth as much. They know they can come back tomorrow and the next day and get a can of beans. The beans are of little value if there is enough to last a year.

The second reason is you don't want people to try and take what you have. If people know you are sitting on a lot of food, water or other supplies, they are going to want to take it for themselves. You are setting yourself up to be robbed and possibly harmed.

Before you go into any bartering situation, know what you have and how valuable it truly is. If you have managed to grow vegetables in the middle of winter, they are going to be more valuable in December than they would be in July. Demand more for you hard work so you can get the items you need without giving away more than necessary.

Valuable Items In An Economic Collapse

As part of your preps for a day when paper money becomes worthless, you will want to invest in certain things that will be quite valuable in the world without money. You want to be able to trade some of your excess for items you truly need. For example; if you have a case of cheap wine that you don't particularly need, trading a bottle of the wine for food, water or medical supplies won't negatively affect you.

You don't need the wine, but you need food. Trading something that is just collecting dust is better than trading something you will need someday.

The following list of items includes things you can stock up on now that are relatively inexpensive. These items may be cheap today, but after the fall, they will increase in value exponentially.

- Alcohol—it can be the cheap stuff, vodka, gin, whiskey
- Chocolate—candy bars, chocolate syrup, powdered chocolate
- Tobacco—cigarettes, rolling papers, loose tobacco
- Medical supplies—bandages, gauze, pain relievers
- Spices—salt, pepper, oregano and so on
- Heirloom seeds
- Personal hygiene items—soap, toilet paper, toothpaste
- Hard candies—extremely cheap! Tootsies rolls and etc...
- Lighters
- Eye glasses—buy a bunch at the dollar store
- Crayons—buy them during back to school sales
- Rope
- Sewing supplies i.e. needle and thread, yarn, knitting needles

Any item that people can eat, drink or satisfy a habit will be valuable. You can never have too much of anything. Every item that is in excess of what you will need or possibly use is going to be your new money. Somebody else will want or need the item and you can use it to barter for what you can use. If you see a great deal on candy, medical supplies or even alcohol, don't pass it up! Add it to your cache of goods and you will be better off for it.

All those old clothes in the attic that you don't like or that are out of fashion, hang on to them if you have the available space. Those clothes can be traded when malls are closed or used for the kids that are growing out of their existing wardrobe. The clothing could be used to make new items, like quilts or towels. Everything will have a use. You don't have to become pack rat, but before you toss anything out, consider a future where an old box of clothes from the 70s would be a boon.

Conclusion

There are plenty of sceptics out there who think prepping for a day when money is worthless is a waste of time. Unfortunately, those sceptics are either ignoring history or choosing to believe otherwise. Whatever the reason, those people are going to be the ones going without because they didn't take the time to prepare for the inevitable. There are plenty of signs indicating the end of the value of the existing currency. The American dollar has decreased in value to the point that even the slightest upset would make it worthless. When that happens, the rest of the nations will fall like dominoes.

Don't worry about people calling you crazy or a conspiracy theorist because you want to prepare for uncertain times. Do what you have to do to protect your family from extremely hard times and possibly starvation. If the death of money doesn't come during your lifetime, that is okay. That is excellent, but it will come and you will feel better knowing your kids will be able to survive it when the situation does come. Learning the skills needed to survive isn't a bad thing. It is a great way to keep your mind sharp while doing something productive.

Don't get caught off guard. Do what you can today to stock up on the necessities that will make your life easier when the world around you is thrust into chaos.

From The Author

Thank you for taking the time to read this book. As an author, I understand the importance of creating books which my readers will find both enjoyable and informative. If you have the time and feel generous, please don't hesitate to leave an honest review of this book..........Ron Johnson

Other Books By Ron Johnson

Prepper's Pantry

In the event of an emergency having an adequate supply of food could mean the difference between life and death!

Are you prepared for any disaster that is about to happen? Do you already have emergency supplies? Is it enough to sustain you and your family's life for an extended period, when help from others would be close to impossible? Have you discussed and implemented the emergency plans with your family?

Fighting for your survival during times of disaster is not about luck, it's about the right knowledge that will help you pull through it. It is all about saving you and your family's life, with the tips provided in this book. Guess what? YOU CAN MAKE IT HAPPEN by reading and following all the guidelines laid out in my book.

The Prepper's Guide To Grid Down Survival

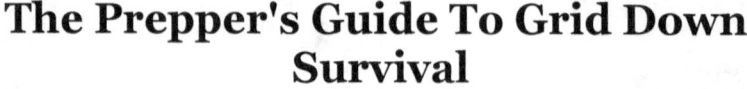

Are you ready to live through a long term downed power grid situation?

Many people don't stop to think how they will eat, get clean drinking water or stay warm when the power goes out. Unfortunately, the possibility of a widespread power failure that extends weeks or months is a very real possibility. This book covers some of the most plausible scenarios as well as how you will manage during the grid failure.

You need to think about how you will maintain personal hygiene, take care of toilet issues and feed your family as well as how you will keep them safe and warm. You don't know how much you rely on electricity until it is ripped away from you. It can leave your entire world turned upside down if you are not ready. It is hard to imagine and prepare for every little thing without doing some research first. This book will hold your hand and help you come up with a plan that will get you through a long lasting grid failure. Planning and preparing can help remove the fear that is associated with the unknown. Get your family involved and start your preparations with the help of the information in this book.

RV Living For Beginners

Are You Fed Up Of Working The 9-5 To Pay The Mortgage Or Rent Plus The Bills And Considering Leaving It All Behind And Hitting The Road?

When you want to change your lifestyle entirely, you need to have enough motivation but you also need to have knowledge about the lifestyle that you are adopting. Many people who want to live in an RV full-time fail to find a balance in their lives which make that living pleasurable, while others can live the dream and learn to compromise on comforts for the sake of freedom. They wake up in the mornings to feel that they have breathed fresh air. They see different scenery every morning if they so wish. What you need to know before joining them is whether you're cut out for the lifestyle and what differences there are between living in a conventional home and living in an RV. This book bridges that gap in your knowledge, and although you may choose to save a fortune by staying at home, you may also choose the lesser traveled road and discover the benefits of living in an RV.

Both lifestyles, either in an RV or a home, have their pros and cons. Many who choose the RV lifestyle find that adapting their lives comes naturally. It takes a unique and free spirited person to compromise on the luxuries of home living in favor of the adventurous lifestyle offered by RV living, though many do. Once you weigh the pros and cons, you can make the choice wisely, and that's what this book is all about. The book will appeal to the free spirited who seek something more than merely surviving month to month oppressed by bills, mortgage payments and housing taxes.

Both have benefits, though those who live the life they choose, rather than the life chosen for them by responsibility, find that RV life tests their personal boundaries and skills freeing up their lives to live beyond the grid. Journey with us and learn if living in an RV will suit you, and be prepared for the journey of your life.

www.ingramcontent.com/pod-product-compliance
Lightning Source LLC
Chambersburg PA
CBHW070729180526
45167CB00004B/1679